RICH DAD'S
ESCAPE FROM THE RAT RACE

How to Become a Rich Kid by Following Rich Dad's Advice

WITHDRAWN

By Robert T. Kiyosaki
with Sharon L. Lechter, C.P.A.

LITTLE, BROWN AND COMPANY

New York ⁓ Boston

Some material in this book is adapted from *Rich Dad Poor Dad: What the Rich Teach Their Kids About Money--That the Poor and Middle Class Do Not!*

Published by Little, Brown and Company in association with CASHFLOW ® Technologies, Inc.

CASHFLOW ® and Rich Dad ® are registered trademarks of CASHFLOW ® Technologies, Inc. Tim, Red and Tina characters are trademarks of CASHFLOW ® Technologies, Inc.

www.richdad.com

Little, Brown and Company

Time Warner Book Group
1271 Avenue of the Americas
New York, NY 10020
Visit our Web site at www.lb-kids.com

First Edition

Library of Congress Cataloging-in-Publication Data

Kiyosaki, Robert T., 1947-
   Rich Dad's Escape From The Rat Race : How To Become A Rich Kid By Following Rich Dad's Advice / By Robert T. Kiyosaki with Sharon L. Lechter; illustrated by Rantz Hoseley.-- 1st ed.
       p. cm.
   ISBN 0-316-00047-7
   1. Finance, Personal--Juvenile literature. 2. Investments--Juvenile literature. 3. Financial security--Juvenile literature. 4. Wealth--Juvenile literature. I. Lechter, Sharon L. II. Hoseley, Rantz, ill. III. Title.
HG179.K5653 2005
332.024--dc22
                                              2004004713

10 9 8 7 6 5 4 3 2 1

LAKE

Printed in the United States of America

LET ME TELL YOU ABOUT A BOOK I READ CALLED *RICH DAD POOR DAD* BY ROBERT KIYOSAKI. ALTHOUGH ROBERT IS RICH AND FAMOUS NOW, IN 1956, HE WAS JUST ANOTHER KID, TRYING TO FIGURE OUT HOW TO MAKE MONEY TO BUY THE THINGS HE WANTED, LIKE COMIC BOOKS AND ICE CREAM.

DAD, CAN YOU TELL ME HOW TO GET RICH?

WHY DO YOU WANT TO GET RICH, SON?

BECAUSE TODAY JIMMY'S MOM DROVE UP IN THEIR NEW CADILLAC, AND THEY WERE GOING TO THEIR BEACH HOUSE FOR THE WEEKEND. HE SAID MIKE AND I WEREN'T INVITED, BECAUSE WE WERE "POOR KIDS."

ROBERT'S DAD WAS A TEACHER. BUT EVEN THOUGH HE WAS REALLY SMART AND HAD A GOOD JOB, HE DIDN'T HAVE MUCH MONEY.

WELL, SON, IF YOU WANT TO BE RICH, YOU HAVE TO LEARN TO MAKE MONEY.

BUT... HOW DO I MAKE MONEY?

WELL, USE YOUR HEAD, SON.

WHICH REALLY MEANT, "THAT'S ALL I'M GOING TO TELL YOU," OR "I DON'T KNOW THE ANSWER, SO DON'T EMBARRASS ME."

SO THAT SATURDAY MORNING, MIKE BECAME HIS FIRST BUSINESS PARTNER.

THE NEXT MORNING, ROBERT TOLD HIS BEST FRIEND, MIKE, WHAT HIS DAD HAD SAID. THEY CAME UP WITH A PLAN.

MIKE HAD GOTTEN AN INSPIRATION FROM A BOOK HE HAD READ, SO THEY STARTED A BUSINESS. FOR THE NEXT SEVERAL WEEKS, MIKE AND ROBERT RAN AROUND THEIR NEIGHBORHOOD, KNOCKING ON DOORS...

... ASKING THEIR NEIGHBORS IF THEY COULD HAVE THEIR USED TOOTHPASTE TUBES.

SOME ASKED WHAT THEY WERE DOING, BUT ROBERT AND MIKE JUST SAID, "WE CAN'T TELL YOU, IT'S A BUSINESS SECRET."

WHEN THEY HAD ENOUGH TUBES, THEY STARTED PRODUCTION.

THE ASSEMBLY LINE WAS CREATED IN ROBERT'S DRIVEWAY.

ROBERT'S DAD AND A FRIEND OF HIS SHOWED UP TO FIND THE PRODUCTION IN FULL SWING.

SEE, BACK IN 1956 TOOTHPASTE DIDN'T COME IN PLASTIC TUBES...

IT CAME IN LEAD TUBES. MELTING THE *LEAD* TUBES WAS THE KEY TO ROBERT AND MIKE'S IDEA OF HOW TO MAKE THEM *RICH*.

CAREFUL....

WHAT'S IN THOSE PLASTER MOLDS?

WATCH...

THIS SHOULD BE A GOOD BATCH.

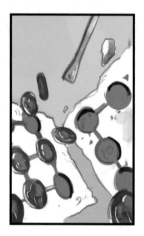

GOOD LORD! YOU'RE CASTING NICKELS OUT OF LEAD!

THAT'S RIGHT!

WE'RE DOING WHAT YOU TOLD US. WE'RE MAKING **MONEY!**

THE FRIEND OF ROBERT'S DAD COULDN'T HELP BUT TO LAUGH AT WHAT THE BOYS HAD DONE.

LET THEM GO! THEY MIGHT BE DEVELOPING A NATURAL TALENT!

...BUT ROBERT'S FATHER SAT THE BOYS DOWN AND TOLD THEM THE MEANING OF THE WORD **COUNTERFEITING.**

GUESS JIMMY AND HIS
FRIENDS ARE RIGHT. WE ARE POOR.

BOYS, YOU'RE ONLY POOR IF YOU GIVE UP. THE MOST IMPORTANT THING IS THAT YOU DID SOMETHING. MOST PEOPLE ONLY TALK AND DREAM OF GETTING RICH. YOU'VE DONE SOMETHING.

I'M VERY PROUD OF THE TWO OF YOU. KEEP GOING. DON'T QUIT.

SO HOW COME YOU'RE NOT RICH, DAD?

BECAUSE I CHOSE TO BE A SCHOOLTEACHER. SCHOOL-TEACHERS REALLY DON'T THINK ABOUT BEING RICH. WE JUST LIKE TO TEACH. IF YOU BOYS WANT TO LEARN HOW TO BE RICH, TALK TO YOUR DAD, MIKE.

MY DAD?

YEAH, YOUR DAD AND I HAVE THE SAME BANKER, AND HE RAVES ABOUT YOUR FATHER.

HE TELLS ME THAT YOUR FATHER IS BRILLIANT WHEN IT COMES TO MAKING MONEY.

THEN HOW COME WE DON'T HAVE A NICE CAR AND A NICE HOUSE LIKE THE RICH KIDS AT SCHOOL?

HAVING A NICE CAR AND A NICE HOUSE DOESN'T MEAN YOU'RE RICH OR THAT YOU KNOW HOW TO MAKE MONEY.

JIMMY'S DAD WORKS FOR THE SUGAR PLANTATION. HE'S NOT MUCH DIFFERENT FROM ME. HE WORKS FOR A COMPANY, AND I WORK FOR THE GOVERNMENT. THE COMPANY BUYS THE CAR FOR HIM. BUT THE SUGAR COMPANY IS IN FINANCIAL TROUBLE, AND JIMMY'S DAD MAY SOON HAVE NOTHING.

YOUR DAD IS DIFFERENT, MIKE. HE SEEMS TO BE BUILDING AN EMPIRE, AND I SUSPECT IN A FEW YEARS HE WILL BE A VERY RICH MAN.

THE THINGS ROBERT'S DAD HAD SAID GOT MIKE AND ROBERT EXCITED AGAIN. AS THEY CLEANED THE MESS, THEY MADE PLANS TO TALK TO MIKE'S DAD THE NEXT SATURDAY.

SO, AT 7:30 ON SATURDAY MORNING, ROBERT CAUGHT T[HE] BUS TO THE POOR SIDE OF TO[WN]

C'MON, FOLLOW ME.

WHO ARE THOSE PEOPLE?

OH, THEY WORK FOR MY DAD.

THE OLDER MAN RUNS HIS WAREHOUSES, AND THE WOMEN ARE THE MANAGERS OF THE RESTAURANTS. AND YOU SAW THE CONSTRUCTION SUPERVISOR WHO'S WORKING ON A ROAD PROJECT ABOUT FIFTY MILES FROM HERE.

DOES THIS GO ON ALL THE TIME?

NOT ALWAYS, BUT A LOT.

SO, WHAT EXACTLY DID YOU SAY TO YOUR DAD?

I ASKED HIM IF HE WOULD TEACH US HOW TO MAKE MONEY.

WHAT DID HE SAY TO THAT?

WELL, HE GRINNED AND SAID HE WOULD MAKE US AN OFFER.

READY, BOYS?

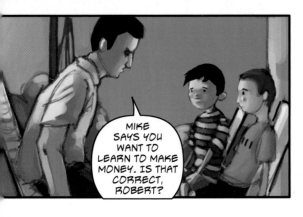

MIKE SAYS YOU WANT TO LEARN TO MAKE MONEY. IS THAT CORRECT, ROBERT?

YES, SIR.

OK, HERE'S MY OFFER. I'LL TEACH YOU, BUT I WON'T DO IT CLASSROOM-STYLE. YOU WORK FOR ME, I'LL TEACH YOU. YOU DON'T WORK FOR ME, I WON'T TEACH YOU.

I CAN TEACH YOU FASTER IF YOU WORK, AND I'M WASTING MY TIME IF YOU JUST WANT TO SIT AND LISTEN LIKE YOU DO IN SCHOOL. THAT'S MY OFFER. TAKE IT OR LEAVE IT.

TAKE IT.

TAKE IT.

GOOD. MRS. MARTIN WILL BE BY IN TEN MINUTES. AFTER I'M THROUGH WITH HER, YOU CAN RIDE WITH HER TO MY SUPERETTE AND START WORKING.

I'LL PAY YOU 10 CENTS AN HOUR AND YOU'LL WORK FOR THREE HOURS EVERY SATURDAY.

BUT I HAVE A SOFTBALL GAME TODAY.

TAKE IT...

...OR LEAVE IT.

I'LL TAKE IT.

PASSING UP SOFTBALL WAS TOUGH FOR ROBERT.

BUT HE KNEW THAT IF IT MEANT HE COULD BE RICH SOMEDAY, IT'D BE WORTH IT.

THE NEXT SATURDAY MORNING, MIKE AND ROBERT WERE WORKING FOR MRS. MARTIN.

SHE WAS A NICE WOMAN AND SAID THAT MIKE AND ROBERT REMINDED HER OF HER TWO SONS WHO HAD GROWN UP.

SHE WAS A TASK MASTER, THOUGH. THEY SPENT THREE HOURS TAKING CANS OFF THE SHELVES AND BRUSHING EACH CAN TO GET THE DUST OFF. THEN THEY HAD TO RE-STACK THEM NEATLY.

IT WAS EXCRUCIATING, *BORING* WORK.

MIKE'S DAD OWNED NINE OF THESE LITTLE SUPERETTES. THEY WERE LITTLE NEIGHBORHOOD GROCERY STORES WHERE PEOPLE BOUGHT STUFF LIKE MILK AND BREAD.

THE PROBLEM WAS, THIS WAS HAWAII--AND IN THE DAYS BEFORE AIR CONDITIONING, STORES COULD NOT CLOSE THEIR DOORS BECAUSE OF THE HEAT.

EVERY TIME A CAR DROVE BY, DUST WOULD SWIRL AND SETTLE IN THE STORE.

SO THEY HAD A JOB AS LONG AS THERE WAS NO AIR CONDITIONING.

FOR THREE WEEKS, MIKE AND ROBERT WORKED FOR THREE HOURS EACH SATURDAY. BY NOON, WORK WAS OVER, AND MRS. MARTIN DROPPED THREE DIMES IN EACH OF THEIR HANDS.

NOW, EVEN AT THE AGE OF NINE IN THE MID-1950S, 30 CENTS WASN'T TOO EXCITING. COMIC BOOKS COST 10 CENTS BACK THEN, SO ROBERT USUALLY SPENT HIS MONEY ON COMIC BOOKS AND WENT HOME.

FOUR WEEKS LATER, ROBERT WAS READY TO QUIT. HE HAD AGREED TO WORK ONLY BECAUSE HE WANTED TO LEARN TO MAKE MONEY FROM MIKE'S DAD, AND NOW HE FELT LIKE A SLAVE.

ON TOP OF THAT, HE HADN'T SEEN MIKE'S DAD SINCE THAT FIRST SATURDAY.

I'M QUITTING! SCHOOL IS BORING AND NOW I DON'T EVEN HAVE SATURDAYS TO LOOK FORWARD TO.

AND ALL FOR 30 LOUSY CENTS!

WHAT? WHAT IS IT?

DAD SAID THIS WOULD HAPPEN. HE SAID TO MEET WITH HIM WHEN YOU WERE READY TO QUIT.

WHAT?! HE'S BEEN WAITING FOR ME TO GET FED UP?

SORT OF. DAD'S KIND OF DIFFERENT. HE TEACHES DIFFERENTLY FROM YOUR DAD. YOUR MOM AND DAD LECTURE A LOT.

JUST WAIT TILL THIS SATURDAY. I'LL TELL HIM YOU'RE READY.

YOU MEAN I'VE BEEN SET UP?

NO, NOT REALLY, BUT... MAYBE. ANYWAY, DAD WILL EXPLAIN ON SATURDAY.

SO, AT EIGHT O'CLOCK THAT SATURDAY MORNING, ROBERT FOUND HIMSELF AT MIKE'S HOUSE AGAIN.

TAKE A SEAT AND WAIT IN LINE.

ROBERT FELT AWKWARD WAITING TO TALK TO MIKE'S DAD, BUT HE WAS DETERMINED TO GET WHAT HE DESERVED, SO HE SAT DOWN AND WAITED.

WAITED 20 MINUTES AS THE OLDER MAN SITTING NEXT TO HIM WENT IN TO TALK TO MIKE'S DAD...

WAITED 40 MINUTES AS THE NICE LADY WHO HAD OFFERED HIM A SEAT WENT IN TO TALK TO MIKE'S DAD...

WAITED UNTIL HE WAS STEAMING MAD-- AND THE ONLY PERSON STILL WAITING.

ROBERT COULD HEAR MIKE'S DAD TALKING ON THE PHONE, RUSTLING PAPERS...

...IGNORING HIM.

FINALLY, AT EXACTLY NINE O'CLOCK, MIKE'S DAD CAME OUT, SAID NOTHING, AND SIGNALED FOR ROBERT TO ENTER HIS OFFICE.

I UNDERSTAND YOU WANT A RAISE, OR YOU'RE GOING TO QUIT.

WELL, YOU'RE NOT KEEPING YOUR END OF THE BARGAIN! YOU SAID THAT YOU WOULD TEACH ME IF I WORKED FOR YOU. WELL, I'VE WORKED FOR YOU.

I'VE WORKED HARD. I'VE GIVEN UP MY SOFTBALL GAMES TO WORK FOR YOU AND YOU DON'T KEEP YOUR WORD.

YOU HAVEN'T TAUGHT ME *ANYTHING*. YOU'RE A *CROOK* LIKE EVERYONE IN TOWN THINKS YOU ARE.

YOU'RE GREEDY. YOU WANT ALL THE MONEY AND DON'T TAKE CARE OF YOUR EMPLOYEES. YOU MAKE ME WAIT AND DON'T SHOW ME ANY RESPECT.

I'M ONLY A LITTLE BOY, AND I DESERVE TO BE TREATED BETTER.

NOT BAD... IN LESS THAN A MONTH, YOU SOUND LIKE MOST OF MY EMPLOYEES.

WHAT?! I THOUGHT YOU WERE GOING TO KEEP YOUR END OF THE BARGAIN AND TEACH ME.

I AM TEACHING YOU.

WHAT HAVE YOU TAUGHT ME? NOTHING! YOU HAVEN'T EVEN TALKED TO ME ONCE SINCE I AGREED TO WORK FOR PEANUTS. TEN CENTS AN HOUR! HAH!

I SHOULD NOTIFY THE GOVERNMENT ABOUT YOU! WE HAVE CHILD LABOR LAWS, YOU KNOW. MY DAD WORKS FOR THE GOVERNMENT!

NOW YOU SOUND JUST LIKE MOST OF THE PEOPLE WHO *USED* TO WORK FOR ME. PEOPLE I'VE EITHER *FIRED*... OR THEY'VE *QUIT*.

HOW DO YOU KNOW THAT I'VE NOT TAUGHT YOU ANYTHING?

WELL, YOU'VE NEVER TALKED TO ME. I'VE WORKED FOR THREE WEEKS, AND YOU HAVEN'T TAUGHT ME A THING!

DOES TEACHING MEAN TALKING OR LECTURING TO YOU?

WELL, UM, YES.

THAT'S HOW THEY TEACH YOU IN SCHOOL, BUT THAT'S *NOT* HOW LIFE TEACHES YOU, AND I WOULD SAY THAT LIFE IS THE *BEST* TEACHER OF ALL.

YOU BOYS ARE THE FIRST PEOPLE WHO HAVE EVER ASKED ME TO TEACH THEM HOW TO MAKE MONEY. I HAVE MORE THAN 150 EMPLOYEES, AND NOT ONE OF THEM HAS ASKED ME WHAT I KNOW ABOUT MONEY.

SO MOST WILL SPEND THE BEST YEARS OF THEIR LIVES WORKING FOR MONEY, BUT NOT REALLY UNDERSTANDING WHAT IT IS THEY'RE WORKING FOR.

SO WHEN MIKE TOLD ME ABOUT YOU WANTING TO LEARN TO MAKE MONEY, I DECIDED TO DESIGN A COURSE THAT WAS CLOSE TO REAL LIFE. THAT'S WHY I ONLY PAID YOU 10 CENTS.

SO WHAT'S THE LESSON I LEARNED FROM WORKING FOR ONLY 10 CENTS AN HOUR? THAT YOU'RE CHEAP, AND TAKE ADVANTAGE OF YOUR WORKERS?

SEE, YOU THINK *I'M* THE PROBLEM. THAT'S WHAT MOST PEOPLE DO WHEN THEY FIND THEY CAN'T PAY THEIR BILLS.

THEY BLAME THEIR BOSS FOR NOT PAYING THEM ENOUGH AND GO LOOKING FOR A BETTER JOB.

SO WHAT AM I SUPPOSED TO DO, JUST TAKE THIS MEASLY 10 CENTS AN HOUR AND SMILE?

THAT'S WHAT THE OTHER PEOPLE DO. JUST ACCEPT A PAYCHECK AND WAIT FOR A RAISE, THINKING THAT MORE MONEY WILL SOLVE THE PROBLEM.

JUST LOOK AT YOUR DAD. HE MAKES A LOT OF MONEY, AND HE STILL CAN'T PAY HIS BILLS.

SO WHAT DO I *DO*, THEN?

YOU NEED TO START USING *THIS*--THE STUFF BETWEEN YOUR EARS.

I *HAVE* KEPT MY PROMISE. I'VE BEEN TEACHING YOU FROM AFAR. AT NINE YEARS OLD, YOU'VE GOTTEN A TASTE OF WHAT IT FEELS LIKE TO WORK FOR MONEY. JUST MULTIPLY YOUR LAST MONTH BY FIFTY YEARS AND YOU'LL HAVE AN IDEA OF WHAT MOST PEOPLE SPEND THEIR LIVES DOING.

HOW DID YOU FEEL WAITING IN LINE TO SEE ME?

TERRIBLE.

AND HOW DID YOU FEEL WHEN MRS. MARTIN DROPPED THREE DIMES IN YOUR HAND FOR THREE HOURS WORK?

I FELT LIKE IT WASN'T ENOUGH. IT SEEMED LIKE NOTHING. I WAS DISAPPOINTED.

THAT'S HOW MOST EMPLOYEES FEEL WHEN THEY LOOK AT THEIR PAYCHECKS. ESPECIALLY AFTER ALL THE TAX AND OTHER DEDUCTIONS ARE TAKEN OUT. AT LEAST YOU GOT 100%.

YOU MEAN MOST WORKERS DON'T GET PAID EVERYTHING?

HEAVENS, NO! THE GOVERNMENT TAKES ITS SHARE FIRST. YOU'RE TAXED WHEN YOU EARN. YOU'RE TAXED WHEN YOU SPEND. YOU'RE TAXED WHEN YOU SAVE. YOU'RE TAXED WHEN YOU DIE.

AS I SAID, THERE'S A *LOT* TO LEARN. LEARNING HOW TO HAVE MONEY WORK FOR *YOU* IS A LIFETIME STUDY.

SO, DO YOU STILL HAVE THE PASSION TO LEARN?

YOU BET!

GOOD. NOW GET BACK TO WORK. THIS TIME, I WILL PAY YOU NOTHING.

WHAT?!

YOU HEARD ME. *NOTHING.* YOU'LL WORK THE SAME THREE HOURS EVERY SATURDAY, BUT THIS TIME YOU WON'T BE PAID 10 CENTS PER HOUR.

YOU SAID YOU WANTED TO LEARN NOT TO WORK FOR MONEY, SO I'M NOT GOING TO PAY YOU ANYTHING.

THAT'S NOT FAIR! YOU'VE GOT TO PAY *SOME*THING.

I'VE ALREADY HAD THIS CONVERSATIO WITH MIKE. HE'S ALREADY WORKING, DUSTING AND STACKING CANNED GOODS FOR FREE.

YOU SAID YOU WANTED TO LEARN. IF YOU DON'T LEARN THIS NOW, YOU'LL GROW UP TO BE LIKE THE PEOPLE SITTING IN MY LIVING ROOM, WORKING FOR MONEY AND HOPING I DON'T FIRE THEM. HOPING MORE MONEY WILL SOLVE THE PROBLEM...

...OR YOU CAN DO WHAT *MOST* PEOPLE GROW UP TO DO – COMPLAIN THAT THERE IS NOT ENOUGH PAY, QUIT, AND GO LOOKING FOR ANOTHER JOB.

BUT WHAT DO I DO?

USE YOUR HEAD. IF YOU USE IT WEL YOU'LL SOON THANK ME FOR GIVING YOU AN OPPORTUNITY, AND YOU'LL GROW INTO A RICH MAN.

NOW, GET OUT OF HERE AND GET BACK TO WORK.

FOR THREE MORE WEEKS, MIKE AND ROBERT WORKED FOR THREE HOURS, EVERY SATURDAY, FOR NOTHING. ROBERT DIDN'T TELL HIS DAD HE WASN'T BEING PAID. HE WOULDN'T HAVE UNDERSTOOD.

OVER TIME, THE WORK ROUTINE GOT EASIER. BUT THEY WERE STILL SAD TO BE MISSING SOFTBALL GAMES AND NOT BEING ABLE TO AFFORD A FEW COMIC BOOKS.

THREE WEEKS LATER, MIKE'S DAD MET THEM AT THE STORE.

HOW'S IT GOING, BOYS?

OK...

YEAH, OK.

LEARN ANYTHING YET?

WELL, YOU BOYS HAD BETTER START THINKING. YOU'RE STARING AT ONE OF LIFE'S BIGGEST LESSONS.

LET'S GO FOR A WALK.

IF YOU LEARN THE LESSON, YOU'LL ENJOY A LIFE OF GREAT FREEDOM AND SECURITY. IF YOU DON'T LEARN THE LESSON, YOU'LL WIND UP LIKE MRS. MARTIN AND MOST OF THE PEOPLE PLAYING SOFTBALL IN THIS PARK.

THEY WORK VERY HARD, FOR LITTLE MONEY, CLINGING TO THE ILLUSION OF JOB SECURITY, LOOKING FORWARD TO A TWO TO THREE-WEEK VACATION EACH YEAR AND A SKIMPY PENSION AFTER FORTY-FIVE YEARS OF WORK.

IF THAT EXCITES YOU, I'LL GIVE YOU A RAISE TO 25 CENTS AN HOUR.

DOESN'T THAT 25 CENTS AN HOUR SOUND GOOD? DOESN'T IT MAKE YOUR HEART BEAT A LITTLE FASTER?

NO.

BUT IT **WAS** TEMPTING TO ROBERT. AT THE TIME, 25 CENTS WAS BIG BUCKS.

OK, HOW ABOUT IF I PAY YOU A DOLLAR, THEN.

NO.

BUT ROBERT'S BRAIN WAS SCREAMING; *"TAKE IT, TAKE IT!"*

OK, $2 AN HOUR.

IN 1956, GETTING PAID $2 AN HOUR WOULD HAVE MADE ROBERT THE RICHEST KID IN THE WORLD.

HE COULD SEE IN HIS MIND ALL THE THINGS THAT KIND OF MONEY COULD GET HIM. A NEW BIKE, A NEW BASEBALL GLOVE, STACKS OF COMICS.

BUT **SOMEHOW** HE MANAGED TO KEEP HIS MOUTH SHUT.

OK, $5 AN HOUR.

W, IN 1956, NOT TOO MANY **ADULTS** MADE AN HOUR. HE KNEW THAT IF MIKE'S DAD WAS ERING THAT MUCH, WHATEVER HE WAS GOING TO TEACH HIM HAD TO BE WORTH IT.

A FEELING OF CALM CAME OVER THEM, AND SUDDENLY THE TEMPTATION DISAPPEARED.

NO.

GOOD.

MOST PEOPLE HAVE A PRICE.

NCE THEY GET THAT FIRST PAYCHECK, THEY START THINKING ABOUT ALL THE WONDERFUL THINGS THEY CAN BUY WITH THE MONEY.

BEFORE LONG, THEY'VE SPENT A LIFETIME WORKING, BUT NOT REALLY UNDERSTANDING WHAT THEY'RE WORKING FOR.

VANT YOU TO AVOID AT TRAP. THAT'S EALLY WHAT I NT TO TEACH U.

I WANT TO TEACH YOU HOW TO AVOID THE RAT RACE. NOT JUST TO BE RICH, BECAUSE BEING RICH DOESN'T SOLVE THE PROBLEM.

IT DOESN'T?

NO, IT DOESN'T.

IT'S LIKE A DONKEY, DRAGGING A CART, WITH ITS OWNER DANGLING A CARROT JUST IN FRONT OF ITS NOSE.

THE DONKEY'S OWNER MAY BE GOING WHERE HE WANTS TO GO, BUT THE DONKEY IS CHASING AN ILLUSION. TOMORROW THERE WILL ONLY BE ANOTHER CARROT FOR THE DONKEY.

YOU MEAN THE MOMENT I BEGAN TO PICTURE A NEW BASEBALL GLOVE, CANDY, AND TOYS, THAT'S LIKE A CARROT TO A DONKEY?

EXACTLY. AND AS YOU GET OLDER, YOUR TOYS GET MORE EXPENSIVE. A NEW CAR, A BOAT, AND A BIG HOUSE TO IMPRESS YOUR FRIENDS. *THAT'S* THE TRAP.

SO, WHAT'S THE ANSWER?

YOU NEED TO OPEN YOUR MIND AND START LOOKING FOR OPPORTUNITIES.

TO LIVE A LIFE DICTATED BY THE SIZE OF A PAYCHECK IS NOT REALLY A LIFE. THINKING THAT A JOB WILL MAKE YOU FEEL SECURE IS LYING TO YOURSELF.

KEEP USING YOUR BRAIN, AND SOON YOU'LL SEE THINGS THAT OTHER PEOPLE NEVER SEE. OPPORTUNITIES RIGHT IN FRONT OF THEIR NOSES.

THE MOMENT YOU SEE ONE OPPORTUNITY, YOU'LL SEE THEM FOR THE REST OF YOUR LIFE.

FOR TWO MORE WEEKS ROBERT AND MIKE KEPT THINKING, TALKING, AND WORKING FOR FREE.

I GIVE THE TOP HALF OF THE COVER BACK TO THE COMIC-BOOK DISTRIBUTOR FOR CREDIT WHEN HE BRINGS IN THE NEW COMICS AND I THROW THE REST OF THE BOOK AWAY.

AT THE END OF THE SECOND SATURDAY, ROBERT SAW MRS. MARTIN CUTTING THE FRONT PAGE OF THE COMIC BOOKS IN HALF. ROBERT ASKED HER WHAT SHE WAS DOING.

HE'S COMING IN AN HOUR.

YOU CAN HAVE THEM IF YOU KEEP WORKING FOR THIS STORE AND DON'T SELL THEM.

AFTER CLEANING OUT THE BASEMENT AT MIKE'S HOUSE THE COMIC BOOK LIBRARY, WAS READY TO OPEN.

WHEN THE DISTRIBUTOR ARRIVED, ROBERT ASKED HIM IF THEY COULD KEEP THE COMIC BOOKS.

THEY CHARGED EACH CHILD 10 CENTS ADMISSION TO THE LIBRARY, WHICH WAS OPEN FOR TWO HOURS EVERY DAY AFTER SCHOOL.

THE CUSTOMERS WOULD READ AS MANY COMICS AS THEY COULD IN TWO HOURS.

IT WAS A BARGAIN FOR THEM, SINCE A COMIC COST 10 CENTS EACH, AND THEY COULD READ FIVE OR SIX IN TWO HOURS.

MIKE AND ROBERT AVERAGED $9.50 PER WEEK OVER A THREE-MONTH PERIOD. THEY PAID MIKE'S SISTER $1 A WEEK TO WATCH THE LIBRARY WHEN THEY WEREN'T AROUND.

THEY KEPT THEIR AGREEMENT WITH RICH DAD AND MRS. MARTIN BY WORKING IN THE STORE EVERY SATURDAY.

THEY ALSO KEPT THEIR AGREEMENT TO THE DISTRIBUTOR BY NOT SELLING ANY COMIC BOOKS.

MIKE'S DAD WAS EXCITED BECAUSE THEY HAD LEARNED THE FIRST LESSON SO WELL. HE HAD NEW THINGS HE COULD BEGIN TO TEACH THEM NOW.

BY NOT GETTING PAID TO WORK AT THE STORE, THEY WERE FORCED TO USE THEIR IMAGINATIONS TO SPOT AN OPPORTUNITY TO MAKE MONEY. BY STARTING THEIR OWN BUSINESS, THEY HAD TAKEN CONTROL OF THEIR OWN FINANCES, AND WERE NO LONGER DEPENDENT ON AN EMPLOYER.

INSTEAD OF PAYING THEM MONEY, MIKE'S DAD HAD GIVEN THEM MUCH MORE.

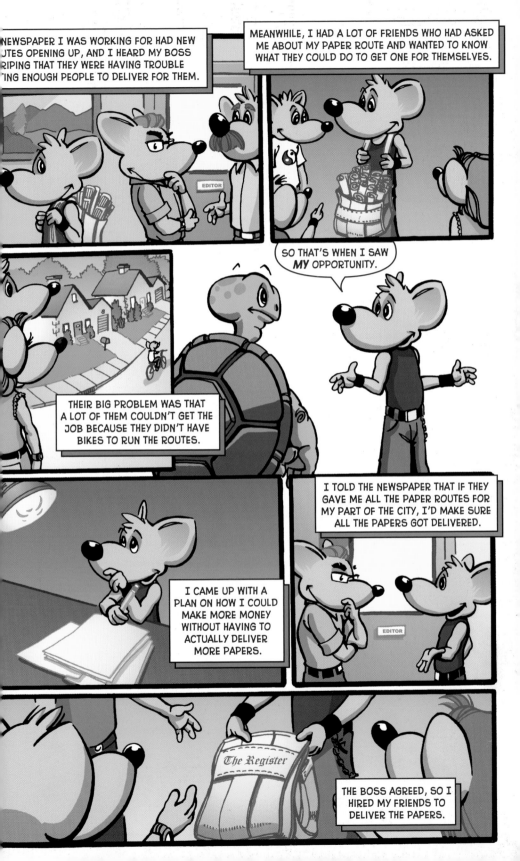

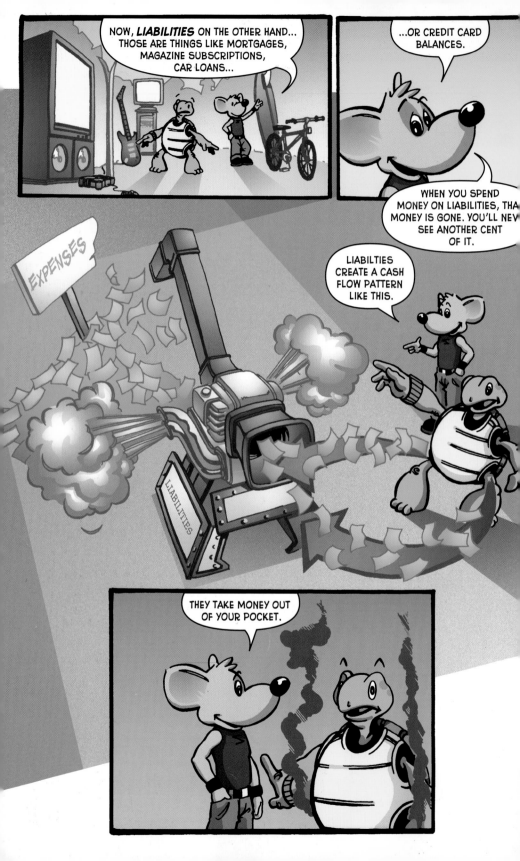

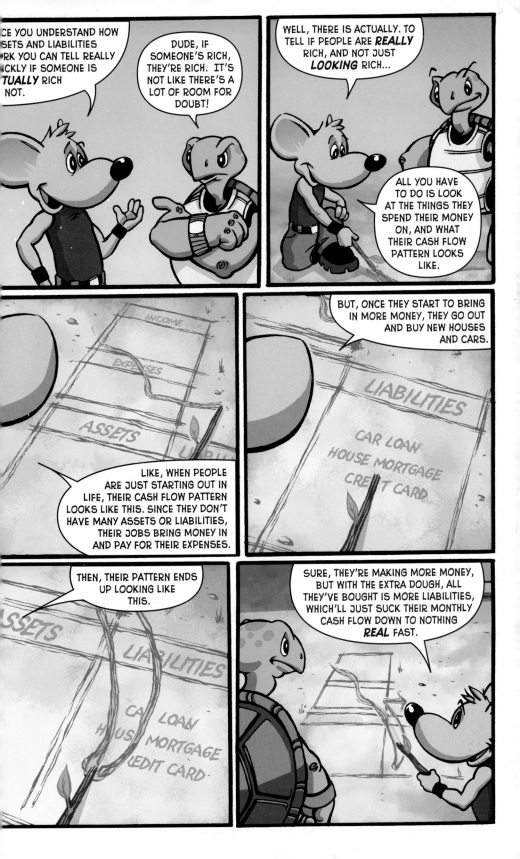

THEY WORK LIKE CRAZY BECAUSE THEY KNOW IF THEY DON'T PAY THEIR BILLS, THEY'LL LOSE ALL THE EXPENSIVE STUFF THEY'VE BOUGHT.

SO WHEN THEY ACTUALLY *CAN* SAVE UP SOME EXTRA MONEY, THEY'RE FREAKED OUT ABOUT DOING ANYTHING WITH IT. THEY'RE SCARED THEY MIGHT LOSE THEIR JOBS AND THAT MEANS THEY CAN'T PAY THOSE BILLS...

SO THEY GET STUCK IN THAT TRAP: SCARED TO DEATH, WORKING LIKE CRAZY, AND NEVER GETTING AHEAD. THAT'S CALLED THE RAT RACE.

NOW, I'M NOT SAYING THERE'S ANYTHING *WRONG* WITH HAVING A JOB.

I WAS ABOUT TO *SAY...*

EVERYONE NEEDS SOME WAY OF GETTING STARTED, AND A JOB IS ONE WAY TO MAKE MONEY AND A GREAT WAY TO LEARN ABOUT A FIELD THAT INTERESTS YOU.

BUT THAT JOB'S NOT GONNA MAKE YOU RICH. IT'S THE THINGS THAT YOU *DO*, LIKE BUYING ASSETS AND NOT RACKING UP A BUNCH OF CREDIT CARD BILLS, THAT'LL MAKE YOU *RICH.*

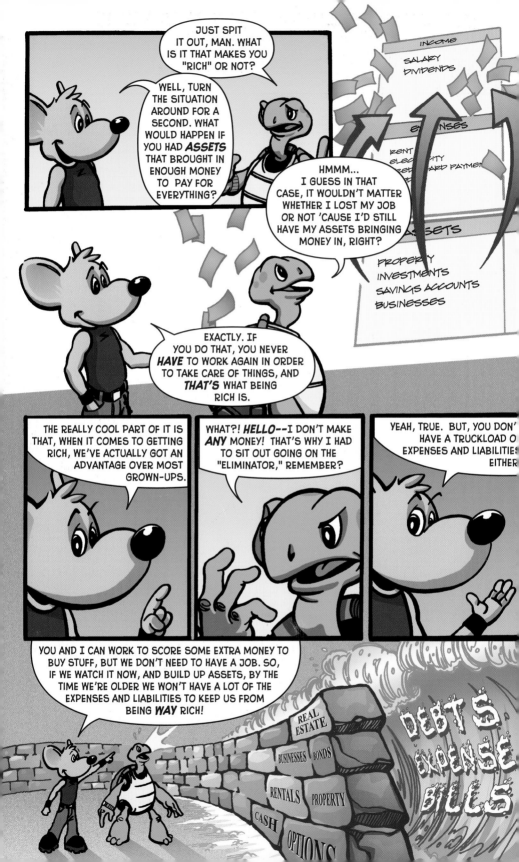

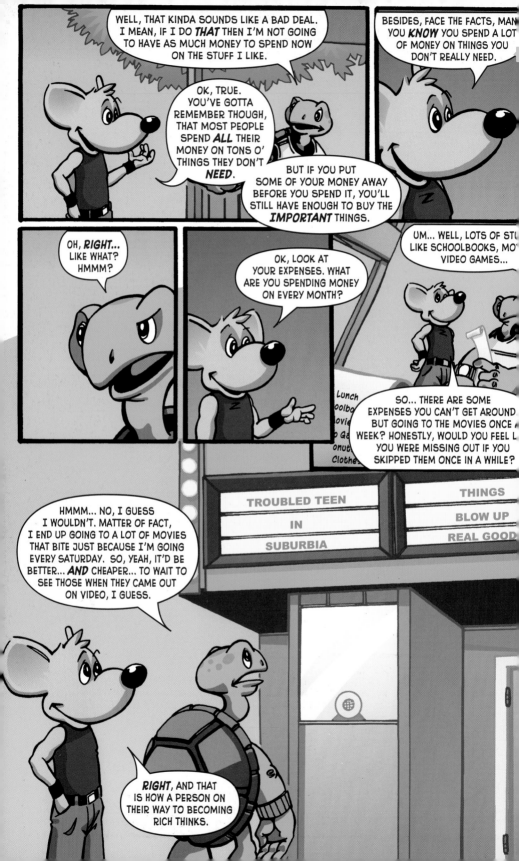

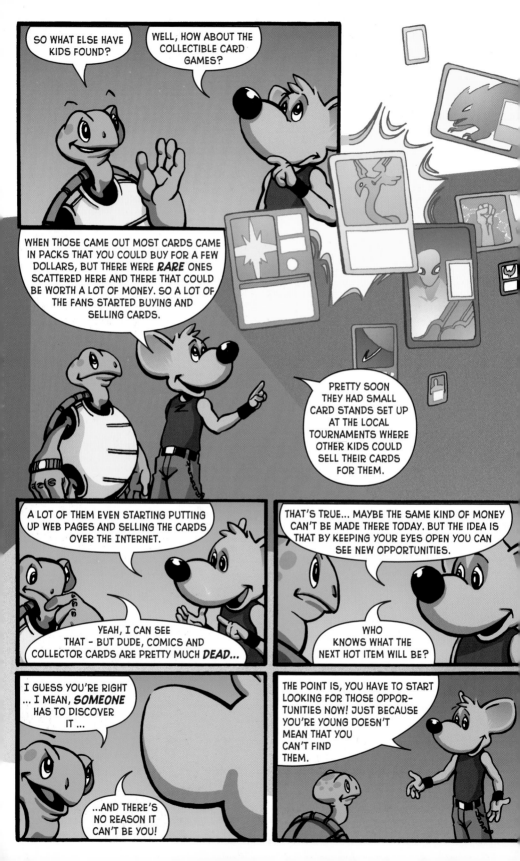

OR, FOR EXAMPLE, YOU CAN TRY TO START YOUR OWN BUSINESS.

WAIT A SEC... YOU WERE STARTING TO MAKE SENSE, BUT THERE'S JUST NO *WAY* I CAN START A BUSINESS.

DUDE, SURE YOU CAN. LOTS OF KIDS OUT THERE HAVE DONE IT.

AND MANY OF THOSE BUSINESSES HAVE BEEN *WAY* SUCCESSFUL BECAUSE KIDS KNOW BETTER THAN ANYONE WHAT OTHER KIDS WANT.

OK, LET'S JUST PRETEND THAT YOU'RE RIGHT. JUST WHAT IS IT THAT I'M SUPPOSED TO START A BUSINESS IN?

WHAT YOU DECIDE TO DO ISN'T AS IMPORTANT AS MAKING SURE YOU'RE ALWAYS LOOKING FOR OPPORTUNITIES.

IF YOU'RE LOOKING AT THINGS THAT YOU'RE EXCITED ABOUT, YOU'RE A LOT MORE LIKELY TO FIND AN OPPORTUNITY THERE BEFORE ANYONE ELSE.

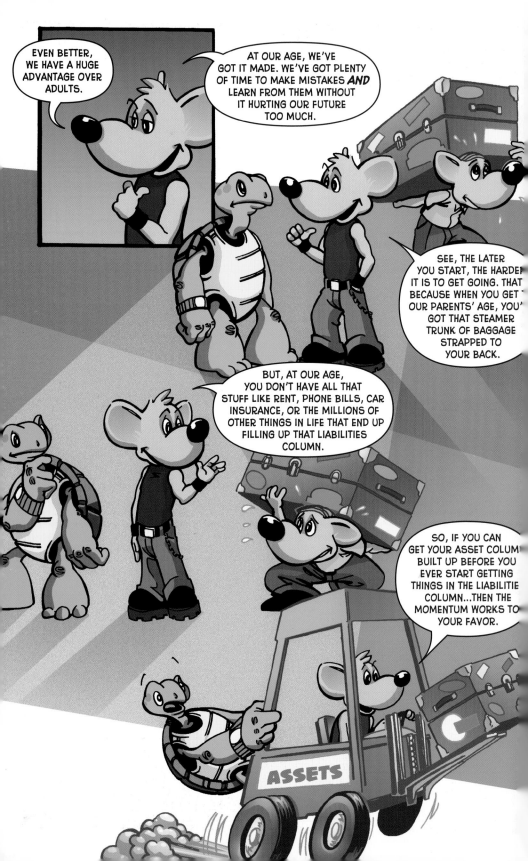

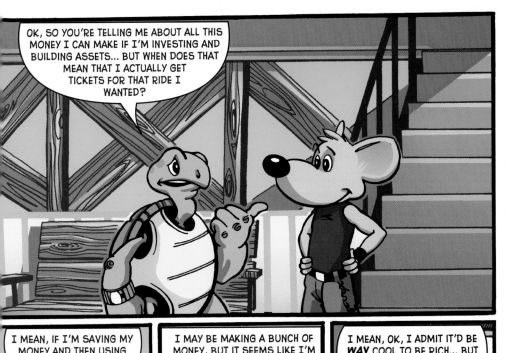

OK, SO YOU'RE TELLING ME ABOUT ALL THIS MONEY I CAN MAKE IF I'M INVESTING AND BUILDING ASSETS... BUT WHEN DOES THAT MEAN THAT I ACTUALLY GET TICKETS FOR THAT RIDE I WANTED?

I MEAN, IF I'M SAVING MY MONEY AND THEN USING THAT MONEY TO BUY MY ASSETS...

I MAY BE MAKING A BUNCH OF MONEY, BUT IT SEEMS LIKE I'M GETTING THE SHORT END OF THE STICK, Y'KNOW?

WITH ALL THAT MONEY GETTING SPENT ON ASSETS, I'M **NEVER** GOING TO BE ABLE TO BUY ALL THE STUFF I WANT.

I MEAN, OK, I ADMIT IT'D BE **WAY** COOL TO BE RICH... BUT WHAT FUN IS BEING RICH IF IT MEANS I END UP MISSING OUT ON EVERYTHING?

LOOK, MAN, BEING RICH AND BUYING ASSETS DOESN'T MEAN YOU **CAN'T** DO THE THINGS YOU LIKE. THE RICH JUST BUY THE STUFF THEY WANT IN A DIFFERENT WAY THAN MOST PEOPLE!

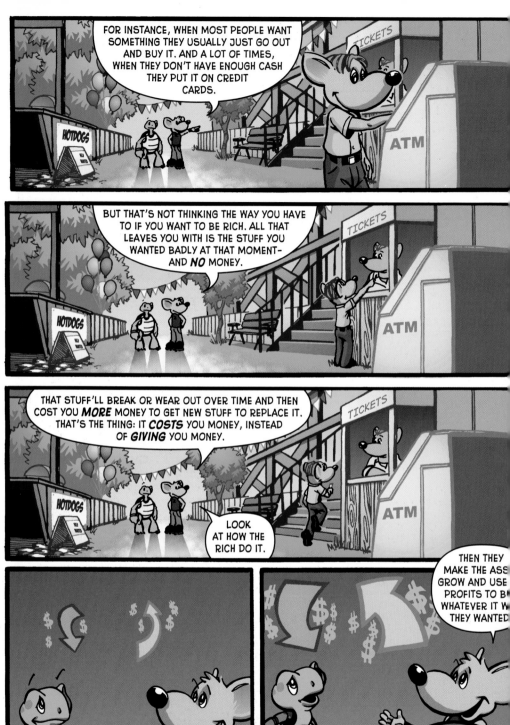

ONE MONTH LATER

TIM! WHATS UP? I HAVEN'T SEEN YOU IN WEEKS, MAN!

HEY RED, SORRY GUY, BEEN BUSY!

IT'S COOL. SO, HOW'VE THINGS BEEN GOING?

IT'S BEEN *SWEET*, MAN! TALKING TO YOU REALLY GOT ME THINKING.

SO, I KEPT THINKING ABOUT A JOB *NOT* GETTING ME THE MONEY I'D NEED TO BE RICH.

RICH?

YEAH-, SO I DECIDED TO START MY OWN BUSINESS.

WAIT A SEC... *YOU* STARTED A BUSINESS?

SO, WAIT A SECOND... YOU WENT FROM HAVING **NO** MONEY A FEW WEEKS AGO TO HAVING YOUR OWN BUSINESS?

YEAH. MY PARENTS EVEN OFFERED TO HELP ME WITH THE REALLY HARD PARTS. THEY WERE REALLY EXCITED WHEN I TOLD THEM I WAS INTERESTED IN MAKING MONEY AND WHAT MY PLAN WAS.

OK, SO WHAT'S THE STORY, RED? SPILL THE BEANS!

SURE, I'LL BE GLAD TO TELL YOU WHAT I TOLD TIM...

YEAH, IT'S **SERIOUSLY** COOL STUFF, BUT THERE'S SOMETHING IMPORTANT WE'VE GOTTA TAKE CARE OF FIRST.

OK, LIKE WHAT?

HMM?

RICH DAD POOR DAD FOR TEENS

THE SECRETS ABOUT MONEY--THAT YOU DON'T LEARN IN SCHOOL!
LEARN HOW TO HAVE YOUR MONEY WORK FOR YOU AND WHY YOU DON'T
NEED TO EARN A HIGH SALARY TO BE RICH. BASED ON THE
BESTSELLING BOOK *RICH DAD POOR DAD*, THIS BOOK IS WRITTEN FOR
TEENS TO COVER ESSENTIAL INFORMATION ON HOW THEY CAN BECOME
FINANCIALLY FREE AT ANY AGE.

CASHFLOW FOR KIDS®

GIVE YOUR CHILDREN THE FINANCIAL HEAD START NECESSARY TO THRIVE IN TODAY'S
FAST-PACED AND CHANGING WORLD. SCHOOLS TEACH CHILDREN HOW TO WORK FOR
MONEY. CASHFLOW FOR KIDS® TEACHES CHILDREN HOW
TO HAVE MONEY WORK FOR THEM.

CASHFLOW FOR KIDS® IS A COMPLETE EDUCATIONAL
PACKAGE WHICH INCLUDES THE BOOK AND AUDIOCASSETTE
TITLED "RICH DAD'S GUIDE TO RAISING YOUR CHILD'S
FINANCIAL I.Q."

CASHFLOW FOR KIDS® IS RECOMMENDED FOR CHILDREN
AGES 6 AND UP.

CASHFLOW® 101

CASHFLOW® 101 IS AN EDUCATIONAL PROGRAM THAT TEACHES ACCOUNTING, FINANCE,
AND INVESTING AT THE SAME TIME...AND MAKES LEARNING FUN.

LEARN HOW TO GET OUT OF THE RAT RACE AND ONTO THE
FAST TRACK WHERE YOUR MONEY WORKS FOR YOU INSTEAD
OF YOU WORKING HARD FOR YOUR MONEY. THE EDUCATIONAL
PROGRAM CASHFLOW® INCLUDES THREE AUDIOCASSETTES
WHICH REVEAL DISTINCTIONS ON CASHFLOW® 101 AS WELL
AS VALUABLE INVESTMENT INFORMATION AND A VIDEO
TITLED "THE SECRETS OF THE RICH."

CASHFLOW® 101 IS RECOMMENDED FOR ADULTS AND CHILDREN AGE 10 AND OLDER.

CASHFLOW® THE E-GAME

WHAT'S YOUR DREAM? FREEDOM OF TIME? UNLIMITED RESOURCES
TO TRAVEL THE WORLD? WHATEVER IT MAY BE, CASHFLOW® THE
E-GAME TEACHES YOU HOW TO GET OUT OF THE RAT RACE AND
ONTO THE FAST TRACK. LEARN ABOUT MONEY AND FINANCES IN A
FUN, INTERACTIVE ENVIRONMENT TO MAKE MORE INFORMED CHOICES
ABOUT MONEY IN YOUR EVERYDAY LIFE!

- PLAY AND COMPETE WITH OTHERS ACROSS THE WORLD IN THE
  ONLINE COMMUNITY THROUGH THE MULTI-PLAYER FEATURE.
- DISCOVER HOW TO BECOME RICH AND FINANCIALLY FREE ON A SMALL OR
  LARGE SALARY!

*TO PLAY THE ONLINE MULTI-PLAYER FEATURE OF CASHFLOW® THE E-GAME REQUIRES THE PUR-
CHASE OF THE CD FOR $99 AND A SUBSCRIPTION TO RICH DAD'S INSIDERS.

ROBERT T. KIYOSAKI

ROBERT KIYOSAKI, PROFESSIONAL INVESTOR, ENTREPRENEUR AND EDUCATOR, WAS BORN AND RAISED IN HAWAII AND IS A FOURTH-GENERATION JAPANESE-AMERICAN. AFTER GRADUATING FROM COLLEGE IN NEW YORK, ROBERT JOINED THE MARINE CORPS AND SERVED IN VIETNAM AS AN OFFICER AND HELICOPTER GUNSHIP PILOT. FOLLOWING THE WAR, ROBERT WORKED FOR THE XEROX CORPORATION IN SALES. IN 1977, HE STARTED A COMPANY THAT BROUGHT THE FIRST NYLON AND VELCRO 'SURFER WALLETS' TO MARKET. AND IN 1985 HE FOUNDED AN INTERNATIONAL EDUCATION COMPANY THAT TAUGHT BUSINESS AND INVESTING TO TENS OF THOUSANDS OF STUDENTS THROUGHOUT THE WORLD. IN 1994 ROBERT SOLD HIS BUSINESS AND THROUGH HIS INVESTMENTS WAS ABLE TO RETIRE AT THE AGE OF 47.

DURING HIS SHORT-LIVED RETIREMENT, ROBERT WROTE THE BESTSELLING BOOK *RICH DAD POOR DAD*. PRIOR TO BECOMING A BESTSELLING AUTHOR, ROBERT CREATED THE EDUCATIONAL BOARD GAME CASHFLOW® 101 TO TEACH INDIVIDUALS IN A FUN WAY THE FINANCIAL AND INVESTMENT STRATEGIES THAT HIS RICH DAD SPENT YEARS TEACHING HIM. IT WAS THOSE SAME STRATEGIES THAT ALLOWED ROBERT TO RETIRE AT AGE 47. THIS ONE-OF-A-KIND GAME IS ALSO IN AN ELECTRONIC VERSION WHICH ALLOWS PEOPLE IN DIFFERENT COUNTRIES TO PLAY AND LEARN TOGETHER ON-LINE.

IN ROBERT'S WORDS: "WE GO TO SCHOOL TO LEARN TO WORK HARD FOR MONEY. I WRITE BOOKS AND CREATE PRODUCTS THAT TEACH PEOPLE HOW TO HAVE MONEY WORK HARD FOR THEM. THEN THEY CAN ENJOY THE LUXURIES OF THIS GREAT WORLD WE LIVE IN."

SHARON L. LECHTER

C.P.A., CO-AUTHOR OF THE RICH DAD BOOKS SERIES, CEO AND CO-FOUNDER OF RICH DAD'S ORGANIZATION, SHARON LECHTER HAS DEDICATED HER PROFESSIONAL EFFORTS TO THE FIELD OF EDUCATION. SHE GRADUATED WITH HONORS FROM FLORIDA STATE UNIVERSITY WITH A DEGREE IN ACCOUNTING AND STARTED HER CAREER WITH COOPERS & LYBRAND. SHARON HELD VARIOUS MANAGEMENT POSITIONS WITH COMPUTER, INSURANCE AND PUBLISHING COMPANIES WHILE MAINTAINING HER PROFESSIONAL CREDENTIALS AS A C.P.A.

TODAY SHE REMAINS A PIONEER IN DEVELOPING NEW TECHNOLOGIES TO BRING EDUCATION INTO CHILDREN'S LIVES IN WAYS THAT ARE INNOVATIVE, CHALLENGING AND FUN. AS CO-AUTHOR OF THE RICH DAD BOOKS AND CEO OF THAT COMPANY, SHE FOCUSES HER EFFORTS IN THE ARENA OF FINANCIAL EDUCATION.

"OUR CURRENT EDUCATIONAL SYSTEM HAS NOT BEEN ABLE TO KEEP PACE WITH THE GLOBAL AND TECHNOLOGICAL CHANGES IN THE WORLD TODAY," SHARON STATES. "WE MUST TEACH OUR YOUNG PEOPLE THE SKILLS--BOTH SCHOLASTIC AND FINANCIAL--THAT THEY NEED TO NOT ONLY SURVIVE BUT TO FLOURISH IN THE WORLD."